THE MERCY OCEAN

[Detail from: Noah. Mosaic in Basilica di San Marco, Venice]

ISBN: 978-1956715897
Library of Congress Control Number: 2022947533

~ ~~~~ ~~~~~~~~~~~~ ~~~~~   ~~~~~~~~~~~~~~~~~ ~~~~~~~~~ ~~~

Vincent A. Salamoni
Missionaries of the Holy Apostles (M.S.A.)

><> ><> ><> ><> ><> ><> ><> ><> ><> ><> ><> ><>

THE MERCY OCEAN
CONTENTS

SAINT VINCENT de PAUL with NOAH

Mosaic in the Basilica of Saint Mark, Venice

The participants of Vincent's retreats were as various as the fishes of the waters.

These people represent the Communion of the Church: young and old, scholar and illiterate, rich and poor, elite and outcasts, clergy and the laity, et cetera.

The sun rise on the evil and on the good, and sends rain on the righteous and on the unrighteous (cf. Matthew 5:45).

Saint Vincent said about his retreats, was like Noah's ark: every kind of creature was to be found in it.

In the one family of God has
THE MERCY OCEAN ...

"USEFUL"

**This is a collection
of information,
which perhaps will be**

HELPFUL TO YOU

AND / OR

OTHERS.

"OCEAN of MERCY"

in the Diary of Saint Maria Faustina Kowalska's
Divine Mercy in My Soul:

I was given the knowledge of the
Heart of Jesus
and of the nature of the fire of love
with which He burns for us and of how

He is an Ocean of Mercy.

(1142)

You expired Jesus,
but the source of life
gushed forth for souls, and the

ocean of mercy

opened up for the whole world.
O Fountain of Life,
unfathomable Divine Mercy,
envelop the whole world and
empty Yourself out upon us.

(1319)

The "Ocean of Mercy" is Jesus' unconditional Love.
"The Mercy Ocean" is a state living in that Mystery.

><> ><> ><> ><> ><> ><> ><> ><> ><> ><> ><> ><>

About:

Vincent A. SALAMONI

He is a member of the Missionaries of the Holy Apostles (M.S.A.). Their charism is to promote, form and accompany vocations to the priesthood and other ministries.

He ministered aboard a dugout canoe in the Peruvian Amazon to served onboard a nuclear air carrier, rather a starship, and retired from in the Chaplain Corps of the United States Navy.

Afterward, he is a Provincial Emeritus of the MSA USA.

He is being through, with, and in, the Mercy Ocean*.

---

* Confer the "ocean of mercy" in Saint Faustina's Diary 1142 and 1319.

><> ><> ><> ><> ><> ><> ><> ><> ><> ><> ><> ><>

✝
DAILY
PRAYERS

INTENTION

**DEAR GOD:
IN YOUR
MERCIFUL PRESENCE
WE PRESENT
TO YOU
OUR PRAYERS,
SUFFERINGS,
THOUGHTS,
JOYS,
ACTIONS,
AND WORDS.
WE ASK THIS
THROUGH YOUR WILL.
AMEN.**

Refer: The Liturgy of the Hours and traditional daily offerings.

OUR FATHER,

who art in heaven,
hallowed be thy name.

Thy kingdom come.

Thy will be done
on earth, as it is in heaven.

Give us this day our daily bread,

and forgive us our trespasses,
as we forgive those
who trespass against us,

and lead us not into temptation,*

but deliver us from evil.

---

* **"and lead us not into temptation"** (cf. Mt 26:41, a liturgical form).
"and do not let us fall into temptation" was translated by Pope Francis.

"It is difficult to translate the Greek verb used by a single English word: the Greek means both 'do not allow us to enter into temptation' and 'do not let us yield to temptation.' 'God cannot be tempted by evil and he himself tempts no one'" (CCC 2846).

Confer:
Catechism of the Catholic Church (CCC),
Part Four Christian Prayer, Section Two,
Article 3 THE SEVEN PETITIONS,
paragraphs 2803-2854.

HAIL MARY,

full of grace,
the Lord is with you!
Blessed are you among women,
and blessed is
the fruit of your womb, Jesus.
Holy Mary, Mother of God,
pray for us sinners,
now
and at the hour of our death.
Amen.

SAINT MICHAEL THE ARCHANGEL DEFEND US IN THE SPIRITUAL BATTLE.

Condensed the prayer *Sancte Michael Archangele*

BLESSED BE GOD

ALL WAYS and ALWAYS.

Glory to

the Father, and the Son,
and to the Holy Spirit:

as it was in the beginning,

is now,

and will be for ever.

AMEN.

———————

SERENITY

ZZZZZZZZZZZZZZZZZZZZZZZZZZZZZZZZZZZZZZZZZZZZZZZZZERENITY

THE SERENITY PRAYER

**God,
grant me the serenity
to accept the things
I cannot change,
courage to change
the things I can,
and the wisdom
to know the difference.**

God, grant me the serenity to accept the things I cannot change, courage to change the things I can, and the wisdom to know the difference - living one day at a time, enjoying one moment at a time, accepting the hardships as the pathway to peace, taking, as he did, this sinful world as it is, not as he did, this sinful world as it is, not as I would have it, trusting that he will make all things right if I surrender to his will - that I may be reasonably happy in this life and supremely happy with him forever.

Philip St. Romain, in *Reflecting on the Serenity Prayer*, was not able to find out how these two versions were evolved from Reinhold Niebuhr's original prayer.

all shall be well - and all shall be well - and all manner of thing shall be well

ALL RIGHT = SERENITY

**No matter how wrong
things seem to be,
they are *all right*.
Things are *all right*
with God and His world.**

All shall be well ...
and all shall be well,
and all manner
of things
shall be well.

Confer: Alcoholics Anonymous and Dame Julian of Norwich

ALL SHALL BE WELL; AND ALL SHALL BE WELL; AND ALL MANNER OF THING SHALL BE WELL. [1]

ALL IS WELL IN GOD'S WORLD AND ALWAYS WILL BE. [2]

Bravo
Zulu [3]

ALL WILL BE WELL. [4]

ALL WELL. WELL DONE. ALL WILL WELL. [5]

[1] "Lord showed in this time – that 'all manner [of] thing shall be well'" (confer: Catechism of the Catholic Church, paragraph 313; The Revelations of Divine Love, chapter 32, 99-100; Dame Julian of Norwich).

[2] "Reflecting on The Serenity Prayer" - Philip St. Romain.

[3] Take my yoke on you, and learn from me; for I am gentle and humble of heart, and you will find rest for your soul" (Matthew 11:29-30). Problems ground life. Bravo, the top maritime pennant when it is alone significance: "I taking in, discharging, or carry dangerous cargo." Zulu, the bottom pennant when alone means, "I requested a tug." May represent Jesus as a tugboat sails together to haul the load. The two pennants hoist together (Bravo Zulu) signifies:

Well done.

[4] "All Will Be Well" (Richard Chilson compiles Julian of Norwich).

"TRANQUILITY"
is not serenity

**The world offers an artificial peace
in a tranquil state without suffering.**

PRINCE of PEACE
WITH the CROSS:
HELP US
TO UNDERSTAND
THIS SERENTIY
WHICH WAS
GIVEN TO US
THROUGH
THE HOLY SPIRIT.

Confer: Pope Francis' Daily Meditations - "Tranquility" is not peace (16 May 2017)

EXPECTATION

"God's mercy is beyond all expectation".
(Saint Leopold Mandić, OFM, Capuchin)

GOD'S PLAN
rather than ours.

(Confer: Matthew 6:10; Romans 8:28)

BE COMFORTABLE
with the
UNCOMFORTABLE.

Comfortable is <u>with</u> the Cross.
(Confer: Pope Francis' Daily Meditations - *"Tranquility" is not peace*; 16 May 2017)

BE REASONABLE ...

we are in
the imperfect world ...
with original sin ...
in a valley of tears!

SERENITY
N O W

ACCEPT
the past.

CHANGE
in the future.

WISDOM
now.

This "Guaranteed Stress Buster" is the prototype of the next page:
"Stress Test with the Serenity Prayer"

GUARANTEED
STRESS BUSTER

I first saw points 1 - 3 of the "GUARANTEED STRESS BUSTER" on a bulkhead (*wall*) in a Navy ship's barbershop, and later added point 4.

The article is intended to make a point.

Hopefully, you have some common sense and will not try steps 1-3.

1.   Place this paper on a solid bulkhead.

2.   Bang head against paper.

3.   Continue until unconsciousness is reached and stress is no longer felt.

OR

4.   Go directly to step 4., eliminating 1-3 and put into practice what the chaplain was hoping you'd do in the first place!

STRESS TEST with the SERENITY PRAYER:

Hopefully, you will have some common sense and will <u>not</u> try steps 1-3.

1. DO NOT ACCEPT THE THINGS YOU CANNOT CHANGE.

2. DO NOT HAVE THE COURAGE TO CHANGE THE THINGS YOU CAN.

3. DO NOT HAVE THE WISDOM TO KNOW THE DIFFERENCE; AND MEASURE FOR A CUSTOM STRAIGHT JACKET!

OR

4. GO DIRECTLY TO THIS STEP.
EVERYONE HAS A HIGHER POWER.
ADJUST YOUR WORLDVIEW.
REFLECT YOUR HIGHER POWER.*

———————

Note:
*   If you are not God, then what is your "Higher Power"?
      Green frogs, music and/or (...).
      Try the loving Supreme Being!

A Supplement of the Serenity Prayer:

GOD,

**GRANT ME
THE *COURAGE*
NOT TO GIVE UP
WHAT I THINK
IS RIGHT
EVEN THOUGH
I THINK
IT IS *HOPELESS*.**

Fleet Admiral Chester W. Nimitz

**If you *can't change*: then *ACCEPT*.
Navigate and steer
the rudder of life with *COURAGE*
and sail in the true course.
Decoded brought *WISDOM*,
and dropped anchor into
the Lord's heavenly harbor!**

(Reverend) *Vincent A. Salamoni*

My *INTENTION*

Mary,
the Mother of God,
in her apparitions in Lourdes
to Saint Bernadette said:
"I do not promise to make
you happy in this world
but in the other."

So, my *INTENTION*
is to practice with the
Serenity Prayer,
as we live
in the valley of tears
within this imperfect world
with its original sin.

CORPUS CHRISTI

The Most Holy Body and Blood of Christ

Anonymous stained glass

**A visit to the
Most Blessed Sacrament
is a proof of gratitude,
an expression of love,
and a duty of adoration
toward Christ our Lord
who is present there.**

Saint Paul VI, *Mysterium fidei* 66;
Catechism of the Catholic Church, paragraph 1418.

Holy Mary,
Our Lady of the
Most Blessed Sacrament,
pray for us.

RP³ =
Learn of the
Real Presence
in the
real presence
of the
Real Presence.

"… could you not
stay awake
with me
for even an hour?"
(Matthew 26:40)

VISIT and RECEIVE

As partakers of Jesus' Divinity,
we humbly visit and receive
the Lord's Body and Blood,
in this *par excellence* mystery.

Jesus' Heart throbs for us,
within the Mercy Ocean!

A SPIRITUAL
VISIT / COMMUNION / HOUR

Have a
spiritual visit
to the Most Blessed Sacrament
and receive a
spiritual Holy Communion.

And even stay for a
spiritual Holy Hour.

The EUCHARISTIC
HEART of CHRIST'S MYSTICAL BODY

**FOR THIS IS MY BODY,
THIS IS THE CHALICE OF MY BLOOD,
DO THIS IN MEMORY OF ME.**[1]

The Sacrament of the Eucharist is a sign and cause of the unity of Christ's Mystical Body ... For there is only one flesh of Our Lord Jesus Christ, and only one chalice unto the union of His blood.[2]

Jesus said: In the Blessed Sacrament, My Heart, which is full of mercy.[3]

The heart of Mary is like the Heart of her Son in all things.[4]

Love is the "heart" of Christ's Mystical Body.[5]

When we are in the state of grace, then we are partakers of the Heart of Christ's Mystical Body.[6]

---

[1] Eucharistic Prayers from the Order of the Holy Mass.
[2] Saint Paul VI, *Mysterium fidei*, 70 and 75.
[3] Saint Faustina, *Diary: Divine Mercy in My Soul*, 1572.
[4] Saint John Paul II, Angelus Message, September 3, 1989.
[5] Saint John Paul II, General Audience, July 8, 1998, paragraph 3.
[6] Confer the Eucharistic Prayers, 2 Peter 1:4 and the Catechism of the Catholic Church, 460.

Stained glass New and Eternal Testament; Pater Karl Stadler, OSB

MOTHER
of
GOD,
pray for us.

HAIL MARY,
full of grace,
the Lord is with you!
Blessed are you among women,
and blessed is
the fruit of your womb, Jesus.
Holy Mary, Mother of God,
pray for us sinners,
now
and at the hour of our death.
Amen.

SUB TUUM

MOTHER OF GOD: UNDER YOUR PROTECTION, DELIVER US FROM ALL DANGERS.

Condensed *Sub tuum praesidium*

Mosaic in Mater Christi Diocesan High School; 1961

**Remember,
O most gracious Virgin Mary,
that never was it known
that anyone who fled to your protection,
implored your help,
or sought your intercession,
was left unaided.
Inspired by this confidence,
I fly unto you,
O Virgin of virgins, my Mother.
To you do I come, before you I stand,
sinful and sorrowful.
O Mother of the Word Incarnate,
despise not my petitions,
but in your mercy, hear and answer me.
Amen.**

Hail, holy Queen,

mother of mercy,
our life, our sweetness,
and our hope.
To you do we cry,
poor banished children of Eve.
To you do we send up our sighs
mourning and weeping
in this vale of tears.
Turn then,
most graciously advocate,
your eyes of mercy toward us,
and after this exile
show us the blessed fruit
of your womb, Jesus.
O clement, O loving,
O sweet Virgin Mary.

Mary, Queen of the Universe, pray for us.

Coronation of the Virgin; Mosaic in Santa Maria Maggiore, Roma

SILENT HEART

SILENT

SILENTIUM

Blessed Virgin Mary; Coptic, 8th Century

SAINT JOSEPH'S LANGUAGE IS SILENCE.

[Confer Saint Pope Paul VI, *Homily for the Feast of Saint Joseph*, 1969]
Solemnity of Saint Joseph, husband of the Blessed Virgin Mary

SAINT JOSEPH: MAY WE RESPECT GOD'S PLAN AND BE PERSONS OF SILENCE.

[Confer: Pope Francis, December 18, 2018]

Silent Heart of Saint Joseph, pray for us.

Try to be
QUIET.
Try
SILENCE
all inner noise,
and
REST
in God's Love.

Compiled from Pope Francis' Apostolic Journey to Mozambique.

SAINT JOSEPH'S FOUR DREAMS:

First dream:

**Joseph was not afraid to take Mary as his wife,
for the child conceived in her is from the Holy Spirit.**

(Matthew 1:20)

Second dream:

Joseph is warned to flee to Egypt.

(Matthew 2:13)

Third dream:

Joseph is told to go to the land of Israel.

(Matthew 2:20)

Fourth dream:

**Joseph is proclaimed to go
to the district of Galilee.**

(Matthew 2:22)

OUR INTENTION
to SAINT JOSEPH

Saint Joseph, according to the Sacred Scriptures, was receiving messages from God while he was sleeping.

Now, we place our **INTENTION** to Saint Joseph.

The second dream: "Flee to Egypt";
13th century mosaic in the Florence Baptistry.

Jesus told us:

"Learn from me, for I am gentle and lowly in heart".

(Mt 11:29)

By his eloquent silence, Saint Joseph imitates Jesus.

— — —

Confer:

PATRIS CORDE

WITH A FATHER'S HEART

7. A father in the shadows

of the HOLY FATHER FRANCIS

Solemnity of the Immaculate Conception of the Blessed Virgin Mary

08 December 2020

ITE ... *GO* TO JOSEPH

Saint Joseph is "an extraordinary figure."

Saint Joseph did not do big things, he had no special gifts; he did not see as a hero in the eyes of those who met him. He was not a famous star: "the Gospels do not report even a single word of his. Still, through his ordinary life, he accomplished something extraordinary in the eyes of God".

Saint Joseph "is an outstanding example of acceptance of God's plans."

Be faithful, in daily routines, because it is the secret of joy.

"May St. Joseph, protector of vocations, accompany you with his fatherly heart!"

— — —

Complied from:
Pope Francis' Message:
"St. Joseph: The Dream of Vocation"; 19 March 2021
World Day of Prayer for Vocations; 25 April 2021

JESUS' CROSS = GOD'S SILENT THRONE

The Sacred Heart of Jesus is the model for the Silent Heart of Saint Joseph.

Jesus's cross is God's silent throne ... let us recognize our limitations, the wounds of our sin. His wounds for our sake. By Jesus' wounds we have been healed.
The risen Jesus bears the marks of the wounds in his hands, feet and side.

These wounds are the everlasting seal of his love for us. All those who experience a painful trial in body or spirit can find refuge in these wounds and, through them, receive the grace of the hope that does not disappoint. Do not be afraid.*

— — —

* Confer: 1 Pt 2:24, Mt 28:5 and Pope Francis; also see St. Joseph in Mt 1:20.

SAINT JOSEPH and HIS ORIGINAL SIN

The Blessed Virgin Mary, the Immaculate Conception, in the instant of her creation was preserved from Original Sin.

Marco Matola, O.F.M., an Italian priest said this in about 1979:

Was St. Joseph removed from Original Sin in his mother's womb?

The friar thought that beautiful idea would be written.

At least, those few words are first printed here in 2021!

Also, in any event:

> Silent Heart of Saint Joseph, pray for us.

— — — — — — — — — — — — —

FLEE / ESCAPE to EGYPT

(Matthew 2:13-15)

There are many things that Jesus did were not written (John 21:25).

Did Joseph want to not walk for health reasons or for safety ones? Could the Magi's gift of gold was used for a better way over the sea?

"Via Maris" (Latin "The Sea Street") is an ancient sea lane, connecting the Holy Land (Israel) to Egypt. Confer Isaiah 9:1 below:

THE WAY OF THE SEA

> Whether any weather or any ways,
> all ways and always
> through, with, in
> *The Mercy Ocean.*

CANTICLE
OF THE
CREATION

¿THE CREATOR EXISTS!

The universe is here.

How it came?

The Creator is.

The Creator had no beginning.
If not another Creator ... another? Nonsense!

Glory to the Creator: as it was in the beginning, is now, and will be for ever.

¿NEXT KNOWING THAT THE CREATOR EXISTS!

After realizing that the Creator exists ...

Is the Creator in the Outer Limits or in the Twilight Zone, or where?

Try promote and foster a relationship for the Creator.

The Creator is a loving One!

BLESSED ARE YOU,

LORD GOD

OF ALL CREATION.

- from the Liturgy of the Eucharist;
Presentation and Preparation of the Gifts

CANTICLE of DANIEL (3:57-87, 56)

Let all creatures praise the Lord
All you servants of the Lord,
sing praise to him (Revelation 19:5).

Bless the Lord, all you works of the Lord; sing praise to him and highly exalt him forever.
Bless the Lord, you heavens; sing praise to him and highly exalt him forever.
Bless the Lord, you angels of the Lord; sing praise to him and highly exalt him forever.
Bless the Lord, all you waters above the heavens; sing praise to him and highly exalt him forever.
Bless the Lord, all you powers of the Lord; sing praise to him and highly exalt him forever.
Bless the Lord, sun and moon; sing praise to him and highly exalt him forever.
Bless the Lord, stars of heaven; sing praise to him and highly exalt him forever.
Bless the Lord, all rain and dew; sing praise to him and highly exalt him forever.
Bless the Lord, all you winds; sing praise to him and highly exalt him forever.

Bless the Lord, fire and heat; sing praise to him and highly exalt him forever.

Bless the Lord, winter cold and summer heat; sing praise to him and highly exalt him forever.

Bless the Lord, dews and falling snow; sing praise to him and highly exalt him forever.

Bless the Lord, ice and cold; sing praise to him and highly exalt him forever.

Bless the Lord, frosts and snows; sing praise to him and highly exalt him forever.

Bless the Lord, nights and days; sing praise to him and highly exalt him forever.

Bless the Lord, light and darkness; sing praise to him and highly exalt him forever.

Bless the Lord, lightnings and clouds; sing praise to him and highly exalt him forever.

Let the earth bless the Lord; let it sing praise to him and highly exalt him forever.

Bless the Lord, mountains and hills; sing praise to him and highly exalt him forever.

Bless the Lord, all that grows in the ground; sing praise to him and highly exalt him forever.

Bless the Lord, you springs; sing praise to him and highly exalt him forever.

Bless the Lord, seas and rivers; sing praise to him and highly exalt him forever.

Bless the Lord, you whales and all that swim in the waters; sing praise to him and highly exalt him forever.

Bless the Lord, all birds of the air; sing praise to him and highly exalt him forever.

Bless the Lord, all wild animals and cattle; sing praise to him and highly exalt him forever.

Bless the Lord, all people on earth; sing praise to him and highly exalt him forever.

Bless the Lord, O Israel; sing praise to him and highly exalt him forever.

Bless the Lord, you priests of the Lord; sing praise to him and highly exalt him forever.

Bless the Lord, you servants of the Lord; sing praise to him and highly exalt him forever.

Bless the Lord, spirits and souls of the righteous; sing praise to him and highly exalt him forever.

Bless the Lord, you who are holy and humble in heart; sing praise to him and highly exalt him forever.

Blessed are you in the firmament of heaven, and to be sung and glorified forever.

CANTICLE of the CREATURES
Laudes Creaturarum (Praise of the Creatures)
Canticle of the Sun
Francis of Assisi; 1225

Most High, all powerful, good Lord,
Yours are the praises, the glory, the honor,
and all blessing.

To You alone, Most High, do they belong,
and no man is worthy to mention Your name.

Be praised, my Lord, through all your creatures,
especially through my lord Brother Sun,
who brings the day; and you give light through him.
And he is beautiful and radiant in all his splendor!
Of you, Most High, he bears the likeness.

Praised be You, my Lord, through Sister Moon
and the stars, in heaven you formed them
clear and precious and beautiful.

Praised be You, my Lord, through Brother Wind,
and through the air, cloudy and serene,
and every kind of weather through which
You give sustenance to Your creatures.

Praised be You, my Lord, through Sister Water,
which is very useful and humble and precious and
chaste.

Praised be You, my Lord, through Brother Fire,
through whom you light the night and he is beautiful
and playful and robust and strong.

Praised be You, my Lord, through Sister Mother
Earth,
who sustains us and governs us and who produces
varied fruits with colored flowers and herbs.

Praised be You, my Lord,
through those who give pardon for Your love,
and bear infirmity and tribulation.

Blessed are those who endure in peace
for by You, Most High, they shall be crowned.

Praised be You, my Lord,
through our Sister Bodily Death,
from whom no living man can escape.

Woe to those who die in mortal sin.
Blessed are those whom death will
find in Your most holy will,
for the second death shall do them no harm.

Praise and bless my Lord,
and give Him thanks
and serve Him with great humility.

A SUMMARY

of the

CANTICLES

[See the following pictures]

(Classical elements: wind, fire, water, earth)

The earth
has
music
for those who
listen

Listen! There are nine (9) birds in the wreath.

PRIMACY of the UNIVERSE

May God grant that I speak with judgment and have thoughts worthy of what I have received, for he is the guide even of wisdom and the corrector of the wise. For both we and our words are in his hand, as are all understanding and skill in crafts.

For it is he who gave me unerring knowledge of what exists, to know the structure of the world and the activity of the elements; the beginning and end and middle of times, the alternations of the solstices and the changes of the seasons, the cycles of the year and the constellations of the stars, the natures of animals and the tempers of wild beasts, the powers of spirits and the reasonings of men, the varieties of plants and the virtues of roots; I learned both what is secret and what is manifest, for wisdom, the fashioner of all things, taught me.

For in her there is a spirit that is intelligent, holy, unique, manifold, subtle, mobile, clear, unpolluted, distinct, invulnerable, loving the good, keen, irresistible, beneficent, humane, steadfast, sure, free from anxiety, all-powerful, overseeing all, and penetrating through all spirits that are intelligent and pure and most subtle. For wisdom is more mobile than any motion; because of her pureness she pervades and penetrates all things. For she is a breath of the power of God, and a pure emanation of the glory of the Almighty; therefore nothing defiled gains entrance into her. For she is a reflection of eternal light, a spotless mirror of the working of God, and an image of his goodness.

Though she is but one, she can do all things, and while remaining in herself, she renews all things; in every generation she passes into holy souls and makes them friends of God, and prophets; for God loves nothing so much as the man who lives with wisdom. For she is more beautiful than the sun, and excels every constellation of the stars. Compared with the light she is found to be superior, for it is succeeded by the night, but against wisdom evil does not prevail. She reaches mightily from one end of the earth to the other, and she orders all things well (Wisdom 7:15-8:1).

In the beginning was the Word, and the Word was with God, and the Word was God ... And the Word became flesh and dwelt among us, full of grace and truth; we have beheld his glory, glory as of the only Son from the Father (John 1:1,14).

He is the image of the invisible God, the first-born of all creation; for in him all things were created, in heaven and on earth, visible and invisible, whether thrones or dominions or principalities or authorities - all things were created through him and for him. He is before all things, and in him all things hold together. He is the head of the body, the church; he is the beginning, the first-born from the dead, that in everything he might be pre-eminent.
For in him all the fulness of God was pleased to dwell, and through him to reconcile to himself all things, whether on earth or in heaven, making peace by the blood of his cross. And you, who once were estranged and hostile in mind, doing evil deeds, he has now reconciled in his body of flesh by his death, in order to present you holy and blameless and irreproachable before him, provided that you continue in the faith, stable and steadfast, not shifting from the hope of the gospel which you heard, which has been preached to every creature under heaven, and of which I, Paul, became a minister (Colossians 1:15-23).

Blessed be the God and Father of our Lord Jesus Christ, who has blessed us in Christ with every spiritual blessing in the heavenly places ... as a plan for the fulness of time, to unite all things in him, things in heaven and things on earth (Ephesians 1:3,10).

* * * * * * * * * * * *

CATECHISM
of the
CATHOLIC CHURCH
(CCC)

Christ is the head of the body, the Church. He is the principle of creation and redemption. Raised to the Father's glory, in everything he [is] preeminent, especially in the Church, through whom he extends his reign over all things (CCC, paragraph 792).

Christ and his Church thus together make up the "whole Christ" (*Christus totus*) [...] Head and members form as it were one and the same mystical person (CCC, 795).

*   *   *   *   *   *   *   *   *   *   *   *

Jesus said to the Holy Apostles:
*Go into all the world
and preach the gospel
to the whole creation* (Mark 16:15).

**St. Francis of Assisi Preaching to the Birds
- Giotto di Bondone (1297-1299)**

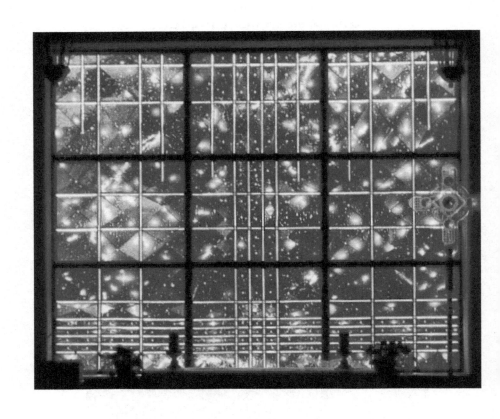

Mary, Queen of the Universe, Daily Mass Chapel; Orlando, Florida

Mary, Queen of the Universe; Edwin Haves (1993)

May all the entire creation, all ways, and in always, praise the King of the universe!

See the Liturgy of Our Lord Jesus Christ, King of the Universe

HEART
of
CHRIST'S
MYSTICAL BODY

HEART
of
CHRIST'S MYSTICAL BODY

SACRED HEART OF JESUS,
HAVE MERCY ON US.

IMMACULATE HEART OF MARY,
PRAY FOR US.

SILENT HEART OF JOSEPH,
PRAY FOR US.

HAND DOWN HEARTS
OF THE HOLY APOSTLES,
PRAY FOR US.

POVERELLO'S
THE KINGDOM OF GOD,
PRAY FOR US.

THE PURE IN HEART,
PRAY FOR US.

GRAFTING HEARTS,
WE TEACH AND ASK
UNITED IN THE LORD JESUS.

AMEN.

COMMENTARY
HEART
of
CHRIST'S MYSTICAL BODY

<u>**The Title:**</u>

HEART OF CHRIST'S MYSTICAL BODY

This title is may be the first time to use this description.

Your and other's heart, when in the state of grace, is united in the Heart of Christ's Mystical Body.

Jesus is the Head of the Mystical Body (see Colossians 1:18). Christ, says St. Paul, the Apostle, is the Head of the Body of the Church.

We see Pope Pius XII writing in the Encyclical Mystical Body of Christ   (Mystici Corporis Christi): The Body of Christ are united with their Head (nn. 11, 14).

A head may be a represent the intellect. Of course, Jesus is the Head of the Body of the Church.

And / both we may represent the heart.

"The spiritual tradition of the Church also emphasizes the *heart*, in the biblical sense of the depths of one's being," where a person decides (Catechism of the Catholic Church [CCC], paragraph 368).

Sacred Scripture is a "reason of the unity of God's plan, of which Christ Jesus is the center and heart (...); we understand the phrase "heart of Christ" (see CCC, 112).

Others hearts are united in the One Heart of Christ's Mystical Body.

SACRED HEART OF JESUS, HAVE MERCY ON US.

A traditional short prayer.

Christ "has loved us all with a human heart. For this reason, the Sacred Heart of Jesus, pierced by our sins and for our salvation" (CCC, 478).

IMMACULATE HEART OF MARY, PRAY FOR US.

A traditional short prayer.

Jesus joined Mary of Nazareth with his sacrifice in her mother's heart (CCC, 964).

Another title of Mary for her heart is a popular prayer that is asking,"Sorrowful Heart of Mary, pray for us."

SILENT HEART OF JOSEPH, PRAY FOR US.

This may be the first use of this term for praying.

Saint Joseph is silent in the Gospels.

HAND DOWN HEARTS OF THE HOLY APOSTLES, PRAY FOR US,

This may be the first use of this term for praying.

"Hand down" is an idiom passing to others.

The Holy Apostles hand down Jesus' teachings (Apostles' Creed).

POVERELLO'S THE KINGDOM OF GOD, PRAY FOR US.

This may be the first use of this term for praying.

"Poverello" is a nickname for Saint Francis of Assisi.
It is famous calling him as the poor one.
We see the Beatitudes (Sermon of the Mount; Matthew 5:3).

St. Francis is a model of the poor in spirit.
The poor in spirit have the kingdom of heaven.

THE PURE IN HEART, PRAY FOR US.

Matthew 5:8 refers it.

This may be the first use of this term for praying.

Temperance is a classical cardinal virtue.

Perhaps, see and pray with other phrases similar **"THE SINCERE HEARTS"**, **"THE UPRIGHT HEARTS"**, **"THE GENTLE HEARTS"**, and **"THE BROKENHEARTED, PRAY FOR US"**!

GRAFTING HEARTS, WE TEACH AND ASK UNITED IN THE LORD JESUS.

This may be the first use of this term for praying.

"Grafting" referred to the True Vine in the Gospel (John 15:5).

We teach because, "The Word became flesh to make us *partakers of the divine nature*" (CCC, 460; 2 Peter 1:4).

We ask because, "it will be given to you; seek and you will find" (Mt 7:7) whatever (Jn 16:23).

The motto of the Society of the Missionaries of the Holy Apostles   (MSA) reflects human hearts to be love to all Creator's children.
(Gal 3:28, 1 Cor 6:17).

UNITED IN THE LORD JESUS.

AMEN.
So be it.

The Most Sacred Heart of Jesus, Solemnity

Confer:
ENCYCLICALS OF POPE PIUS XII
HAURIETIS AQUAS
on devotion to the Sacred Heart
and
MYSTICI CORPORIS
of the Mystical Body

Also see: **The encyclical REDEMPTOR HOMINIS, which Saint John Paul II explained the theme of unity of Mary's Immaculate Heart with the Sacred Heart.**

THE SACRED HEART of JESUS
is not the only one part of the Heart of Christ's Mystical Body?

Is the Immaculate Heart
of the Blessed Virgin Mary,
is the Silent Heart of Joseph,
and all the hearts of the partakers
of Jesus' Divinity
are part of the
Heart of Christ's Mystical Body?

80

Where is
YOUR

part of the
Heart of Christ's
Mystical Body?

Holy Mary, Mother of the Heart of Christ's Mystical Body, pray for us.

From the open heart
of the Crucified One,
God's love reaches
each one of us.
Let us allow His gaze
to rest on us.
We will understand
that we are not alone,
but loved,
for the Lord
does not abandon us
and He never,
ever forgets us.

Franciscus
General Audience; 8 April 2020

LET US PRAY

Father,
help us to
seek
the values that will bring us
lasting joy in this changing world.
In our desire for what you promise
make us one in mind and heart.
Grant this through our
Lord Jesus Christ, your Son,
who lives and reigns with you and
the Holy Spirit,
one God, for ever and ever.
– Amen.

Twenty-First Week in Ordinary Time,
Liturgy of the Hours, Office of Readings,
Concluding Prayer

From a quote of
Saint Jane Frances de Chantal
and from
THE MERCY OCEAN.

"Sometimes put yourself very simply before God, certain of his presence everywhere, and without any effort, whisper very softly to His sacred heart whatever your own heart prompts you to say." - (Letters of Spiritual Direction)

Present in the Merciful Presence.
Present to the Sacred Heart
the encouragement was given.

Saint Jane Frances de Chantal's
LITTLE BOAT

"Here is a little model of what we should do when we are taken by surprise as we row peacefully in our little boat. When all our emotions arise to stir up a great internal storm that seems certain to overwhelm us or drag us after it, we must not wish to calm this tempest ourselves. Rather, we must gently draw near the shore, keeping our will firmly in God, and coast along with the little waves; by humble knowledge of ourselves, we will reach God, who is our sure port. Let us go gently along without agitation or anxiety and without giving in to our emotions."

˗ (St. Jane de Chantal: Exhortations, Conferences and Instructions)

STELLA MARIS

DEEP WATER

Hail Mary,
full of grace, the Lord is with you!
Blessed are you among women,
and blessed is the fruit of your womb, Jesus.

(Litany)

<u>HOLY MARY</u>

MOTHER of GOD,

STAR of the SEA,

QUEEN of the HOLY APOSTLES,

QUEEN of SEAFARERS,

QUEEN of FISHERS,

QUEEN of FAIR WINDS,

QUEEN of FOLLOWING SEAS,

QUEEN of the UNIVERSE,

PRAY FOR US

sinners, now and at the hour of our death.

Amen.

MARY, STAR of the SEA,
light of every ocean, guide seafarers across all dark and stormy seas that they may reach the haven of peace and light prepared in Him who calmed the sea. As we set forth upon the oceans of the world and cross the deserts of our time, show us, O Mary, the fruit of your womb, for without your Son we are lost. Pray that we will never fail on life's journey, that in heart and mind, word and deed, in days of turmoil and in days of calm, we will always look to Christ and say, 'Who is this that even wind and sea obey him?'

Our Lady of Peace, pray for us!

Bright Star of the Sea, guide us!

Our Lady, Star of the Sea, pray for seafarers, pray for us.

[The prayer of Saint Pope John Paul II to Our Lady Star of the Sea]

MESSAGE OF HIS HOLINESS POPE FRANCIS
FOR THE 2020 WORLD DAY OF VOCATIONS
(The Last Two Paragraphs)

Even amid the storm-tossed waters, then, our lives become open to praise. This is the last of our vocation words, and it is an invitation to cultivate the interior disposition of the Blessed Virgin Mary. Grateful that Lord gazed upon her, faithful amid fear and turmoil, she courageously embraced her vocation and made of her life an eternal song of praise to the Lord.

Dear friends, on this day in particular, but also in the ordinary pastoral life of our communities, I ask the Church to continue to promote vocations. May she touch the hearts of the faithful and enable each of them to discover with gratitude God's call in their lives, to find courage to say "yes" to God, to overcome all weariness through faith in Christ, and to make of their lives a song of praise for God, for their brothers and sisters, and for the whole world. May the Virgin Mary accompany us and intercede for us.

Franciscus

STORMY SEAS

PAIN:
A Storm.
GRATITUDE:
In the same boat.
ENCOURAGE:
Don't worry.
PRAISE:
Live the song of
the Star of the Sea.

Confer:
**MESSAGE OF HIS HOLINESS POPE FRANCIS
FOR THE 2020 WORLD DAY OF VOCATIONS**

MESSAGE OF HIS HOLINESS POPE
FRANCIS
FOR THE CELEBRATION OF THE
54th WORLD DAY OF PEACE
1 JANUARY 2021

A CULTURE OF CARE AS A PATH TO PEACE

9. There can be no peace without a culture of care

At a time like this, when the barque of humanity, tossed by the storm of the current crisis, struggles to advance towards a calmer and more serene horizon, the "rudder" of human dignity and the "compass" of fundamental social principles can enable us together to steer a sure course. As Christians, we should always look to Our Lady, Star of the Sea and Mother of Hope. May we work together to advance towards a new horizon of love and peace, of fraternity and solidarity, of mutual support and acceptance.

Our Lady, Star of the Sea and Mother of Hope, pray for us.

A BEACON of HOPE

The Cross is like a beacon that point out the port to ships that are still afloat on stormy seas. It is the sign of the hope that does not let us down; and it tells us that not even one tear, not one cry is lost in God's saving plan.

Confer: Francis, Bishop of Rome, General Audience, March 31, 2021

Have hope,
an anchor
of the soul,
set and secure.

(confer Hebrews 6:19)

Stained glass in Mater Christi Chapel, Astoria NY

**In the midst of this storm
I cast my anchor
toward the throne of God,
the anchor that is the lively home in my heart.
(Saint Paul Le-Bao-Tinh, Vietnamese Martyrs)**

STILLA MARIS
A Drop of the Sea*

The Blessed Virgin Mary has various titles and here are two:

STELLA MARIS - the Star of the Sea.

STILLA MARIS - a Drop of the Sea.

Perhaps would be useful to study about Eusebius of Caesarea, Saint Jerome, the given name Miriam, the name of Mary, Ave Maria, Stella Maris, and confer Saint Faustina's Divine Mercy in My Soul (*Diary*, 432) and in other places.

Be immersed in fathomless Divine Mercy
like a drop of water in the ocean.

HOLY MARY,
a Drop of the Sea,
pray for us.

---

* Some biblical scholars have seen in it the Hebrew words mar (bitter) and yam (sea). This first meaning can refer to Mary's bitter suffering at the cross and her many tears of sorrow.
Another interpretation of the word mar renders Mary's name to mean "drop of the sea" and St. Jerome rendered it in Latin as stilla maris, which was later changed to stella (star) maris. This accounts for a popular title for Mary as "Star of the Sea".
Furthermore, perhaps study for the Pole Star (Polaris, North Star, polar star, polestar), which was related with earlier Marian veneration.

OUR LADY of MOUNT CARMEL = STELLA MARIS

The veneration of Our Lady of Mount Carmel, often is associated with the devotion of her title Stella Maris.

As seen, the Brown Scapular is not holding here, rather the Carmelite's coat of arms, which includes stars.

Perhaps, a star there recalls the relationship with Our Lady, Star of the Sea; as we know the sanctuary Stella Maris in Mount Carmel.

The MOTHER of GOD

is the source of all her titles.

**Words have limitations.
These "lifesaver" and "beacon"
are catalysts for devotion to her.**

The Magi from the East followed the Child's star.

**The Mother of God
has a title
STELLA MARIS | the STAR of the SEA.**

We follow her.

**In our lives,
we become overwhelm
in the waves of our lives.**

We look to her as a lifesaver for us.

**Our Mother is a beacon
beckons to:**
The lamp is the Lamb.

* "The lamp is the Lamb" (Revelation 21:23).

After the Nativity of the Lord,
the Magi's gifts were presented
to the Wedding of Cana!

Time is a measure.

In eternity there is no time.
With the Lord one day is like a thousand years,
and a thousand years are like one day.

The history of these mysteries are partially unveiled here:

The Star of Bethlehem and the Star of the Sea
are beacons that beckon to:
the lamp is the Lamb.

LAMB of GOD ... AGNUS DEI.

Saint Bonaventure noted that Our Lady, the Star of the Sea: "guides to a landfall in heaven those who navigate the sea of this world in the ship of innocence or penance."

The Blessed Virgin Mary is a beacon and a lifesaver in our stormy seas.

PSALM 23 (Nautical Version)

The Lord of the Seas,
there is nothing I shall requisition.
Peaceful, like glass are the waters
where he gives me rack time.
To restful ports he leads me,
to boost my low morale.

He guides me along the true course;
he is faithful to his name.
If I should sail into storms of darkness
no shipwreck would I fear.
You are there with your chart and compass;
with these you give me liberty.

You have set up the mess decks for me
in the sight of my foes.
You anoint my head with a trim;
my mug is overflowing.

Surely fair winds and following seas
shall follow me all the days of my cruise.
In the Lord's own harbor shall I moor
for ever and ever.

[The insignia is from the radar navigation's rich history.]

SPIRITUAL NAVIGATION

Navigators speak of a "three point fix" in order to be able a reliable position on a chart. It is when three distances intersect themselves.

In a discernment is a "spiritual triangulation".

Spiritually also needs to intersect three points together.

For finding your correct position after ponder:

1. God's objective moral law, revealed in Sacred Scripture, Tradition and a legitimate magisterium;
2. God arranges providentially in situations; and
3. the testimony of your own informed conscience and inner peace.

By lining up all three points at the same time is to be prudent.
It is the only way to stay as close to the course as we need.

If in a decision giving ALONE:
a) Objective law alone is to run aground on LEGALISM.
b) Situations alone is to drift aimlessly into RELATIVISM.
c) Individual conscience alone is to sink into SUBJECTIVISM.

In the event: "To navigate is precise; to live is not precise."

We need all the help in the voyage of life!

SAINT PETER WALKED on the WATER
Matthew 14:22-36

Peter got out of the boat and began to walk on the water toward Jesus.

(...) he became frightened; and, beginning to sink (...)

(...) Peter cried out in an act, "LORD, SAVE ME!"
Immediately Jesus stretched out his hand and caught him (...)

What happened when Peter was caught, *before* he got into the boat?

After sinking:
Did Peter became a playing ball, which Jesus had caught?
Did Peter became a hauling fish, whom did Jesus dragged to the boat?
Did Peter walk on water, after his act of faith?

Saint Peter walked on the water!

VINCENT de PAUL
Royal Chaplain of the Galleys of France

Vincent consoled the sorrowful, defended the rights of orphans and generously aided widows; whatever he did for the least, he did for Jesus.

The miserable condemned prisoners aboard the galleys were especially the least ... targets for opportunities to receive spiritual and corporal works of mercy.

They endured in various circumstances: damp dungeons ... chains on their legs ... only black bread and water ... covered with vermin and ulcers ... more repulsive conditions!

In any event, his legacy includes that King Louis XIII appointed him the royal almoner of the galleys.

The best title of Vincent de Paul is:

SAINT

**Saint Elizabeth Ann Seton,
the Patroness of the Sea Services**

THE NAVY LINK

SAINT ELIZABETH ANN SETON was canonized in September 14, 1975 by Pope Paul VI. Shortly the then Chief of Navy Chaplains, Monsignor John J. O'Connor (formerly John Cardinal O'Connor, the Archbishop of New York) took the initiative to proclaim Mother Seton "PATRONESS OF THE SEA SERVICES" for Catholic men and women in uniform the Navy, the Marine Corps, the Coast Guard, and the Merchant Marine. Admiral James D. Watkins, then Chief of Naval Personnel, collaborated closely with Rear Admiral O'Connor in that effort and in 1977 they struck a medal honoring Mother Seton because of her link to the Navy through her two sons, William and Richard.

* * * * * * * * * * * *

William Seton was appointed Midshipman on the fourth of July in 1817. In February of 1818 he reported for duty aboard the USS INDEPEN-DENCE, and in July he was assigned to the USS MACEDONIAN which sailed from Boston later in the year on a cruise around Cape Horn to Valparaiso, Chile. While he was on this voyage, his mother died on January 4, 1821. In May of 1822 he was ordered to the USS CYANE. This voyage in the Mediterranean and along the coast of Africa lasted more than three years. Late in February of 1826 he was given his commission as Lieutenant in the U.S. Navy. In November he was ordered to the Sloop of War HORNET which was sent from Norfolk, Virginia to cruise the West Indian waters in search of pirates. He resigned as Lieutenant on July 5 of 1834, almost seventeen years to the day he was appointed Midshipman.

* * * * * * * * * * * *

Richard Seton, the second son, was the Captain's clerk on the USS CYANE. The Navy has very little information to give about Richard Seton. For almost a year (June 1822 to April 1823), he was on duty with this ship off the coast of Africa, where the United States Government was supporting the American Colonizing Society in its efforts to found a free Negro Colony in Liberia. In a letter from the Reverend Jehudi Ashmun, an Episcopalian missionary in the area, we learn that Richard contracted a fatal fever while nursing the minister back to life. Shortly afterwards, Richard Seton died of this fever on June 26 of 1823 and was buried at sea.

* * * * * * * * * * * *

This as far as know now is the best source:

In 2011 "The 'Navy Link' to St. Elizabeth Ann Seton" was found in a website famvin.org

At 2021, further information here was not found in domain public sites, and about this information.

* * * * * * * * * * * *

SAINT ELIZABETH ANN SETON, PATRONESS OF THE SEA SERVICES, PRAY FOR US.

* * * * * * * * * * * *

SAINT JOHN BOSCO
with
THE MERCY OCEAN

**Saint John Bosco's Vision of
Two Pillars: Holy Eucharist and Our Lady**

Behold, I have given you authority to tread upon serpents and scorpions, and over all the power of the enemy; and nothing shall hurt you.

(Luke 10:19)

Confer: United States Navy Jack; circa 1775

GUIDE
FISHING
for
PEOPLE

><>

Jesus, the versatile carpenter said,
I AM THE GOOD SHEPHERD.
(John 10:14)

Also, Jesus is the:

DIVINE FISHER.

DIVINE CATCHING

"So Simon Peter went aboard and hauled the net ashore, full of large fish, a hundred fifty-three of them; and though there were so many the net was not torn" (John 21:11).

The Call of the Apostles, Fishers of Men; Duccio di Buoninsegna

Some ancients thought that the number of 153 fishes were representing for all of their species, and this haul was a symbol for all people.

**Jesus said to His Holy Apostles,
"You will be catching people."**
(Luke 5:10)

The **Sermon of Saint Anthony to the Fish**
was because the people did not listen
to the Word of God.

O ye fishes of the sea and of the river be attentive rather the people!

[*I Fioretti* of Saint Francis of Assisi, chapter 40]

Saint Anthony Preaching to the Fishes, ca. 1630, attributed to Francisco de Herrera the Elder

"The Good Shepherd has risen, who laid down his life for his sheep and willingly died for his flock, alleluia."
(The Holy Mass, Monday of the Third Week of Easter; Entrance Antiphon)

The Divine Fisher has risen, who laid down his life for his people and willingly died for his catch, alleluia.
(poetic license)

(Saint Peter University Hospital, Brunswick NJ USA; stained glass)

The Divine Fisher has risen.
He caught his people and died for them.
(Confer Luke 5:1-10, John 21:11)

**For the kingdom of heaven is like
a fisher who went out early
in the morning to hire a crew.**
Confer: Matthew 20:1

There are vocations
AT ALL TIMES
In Every Age*
and follow to them!

---

* AT ALL TIMES In Every Age - E. M. MENARD

The Society of the Missionaries of the Holy Apostles was first founded* in the Apostolicus Vicariatus Sancti Iosephi de Amazones.

"For my yoke is easy, and my burden is light."
Matthew 11:30

The Arapaima gigas (paiche) fish is hauled by a local fisher.

* Eusebe M. Menard, O.F.M.
   Founder of the Society of the Missionaries of the Holy Apostles (M.S.A.)

The Miraculous Catch of Fish; Jan Toorop, 1912, Netherlands

Rather fish ... FISHING for PEOPLE:

CAST into the DEEP ...
catching people (Luke 5:1-10).

The Society of the Missionaries of the Holy Apostles (M.S.A.)

Charism:

PROMOTE, FORM and ACCOMPANY

VOCATIONS

to the priesthood and other ministries in the Church.

PRAY FOR VOCATIONS!

The argonauts ... any sailor ... or any person ...
be tempted from the sirens ... or any reason ...
don't lure to the rocky coast for a shipwreck ...
if there is in a collision ... hopefully, then repair it.

———————

The SACRAMENT of PENANCE
within
THE MERCY OCEAN

[Spiritual Barnacles]

CULINARY:
Barnacles are crustaceans related to crabs, lobsters, and shrimps.
They are edible as a delicacy in Spanish, Portuguese ports, and even NYC, which is the capital of the world.

NAUTICAL:
Barnacles may attach in a ship's hull, which drags their speed.
There are tales about keelhauling, which is a form of penance. A culpable mariner was dragged over the barnacles.
Some sailors after keelhauled would not tale that sea story because they lost their life there!

CHURCH:
Many times persons write about the Church as a ship; as individuals are like a ship.
Barnacles are not here; a hull has to been cleaned.
If stay; they impede us. We want to be safe and not smash to a coastal rock.
Peter, the rock that Jesus built his church ... Lord save us, or we perish!

**The PASSION of JESUS
is a
SEA of SORROWS
but it is also an
OCEAN of LOVE.**

**Ask the Lord
to teach you to
FISH in this OCEAN.**

DIVE into its DEPTHS.

**NO MATTER HOW DEEP YOU GO,
YOU WILL
NEVER REACH THE BOTTOM.**

(Saint Paul of the Cross)

As we learning to *never reach the bottom:*
In her voyage across the ocean of this world, the Church is like a great ship being pounded by the waves of life's different stresses. Our duty is not to abandon ship but to keep her on course. (Saint Boniface)
(...) and the storms the ship of Peter has weathered because it has Christ on board. (Saint Thomas Becket)

PEACE

You are anxious and worried about many things.

(Saint Luke 10:41)

PRAY, HOPE, and DON'T WORRY.

A STATUE of SAINT PIUS
is on the floor of
THE MERCY OCEAN.

There is a statue of Saint (aka Padre Pio) Pius of Pietrelcina at the bottom of the waters ... its location is near the Tremiti Island, which is north the spur of the heel, along the southern east coast of the Italian boot. This devotional art, even in the midst of storms is a memorial of that native son in that not distant area.

(Cf: Bret Thomas, OFS; 07/11/2021. The photo source: Antonio84; twitter.com)

PRAY, HOPE, AND DON'T WORRY ET CETERA

Pray, hope, and don't worry.
Worry is useless.
God is merciful
and will hear your prayer.
Prayer is the best weapon we possess.
It is the key that opens the heart of God.
(Saint Padre Pio of Pietrelcina)

— — —

SAIL in a

CALM ZONE: SILENT PEACE

with the Creator of the Seas
in any conditions, including agitation waters and any storms.*

— — —

* The principle source is this sentence: [Entry April 1 - *Padre Pio's Spiritual Direction for Every Day*, edited by Gianluigi Pasquale; translated by Marsha Daigle-Williamson. Originally published in Italian as *365 Giorni con Padre Pio* by Edizioni San Paolo S.R.L.-Cinisello Balsamo (MI)]:
"Be at peace in all things, because the enemy, who always fishes in troubled waters, takes advantage of our discouragement to achieve his intentions more readily."
It was transfigured with the spirit of others, as this is in *THE MERCY OCEAN*.

Also entries are April 16, May 7 and 16:

Jesus' heart and mine were fused together - (...)
No longer were there two hearts beating but only one.
My heart had disappeared,
like a drop of water that is engulfed in the sea.
The sea of paradise was Jesus, the King.

"Thy will be done, / On earth as it is in heaven" [Matthew 6:10]. (...) "Repeat them even when you are engulfed in the ocean of Jesus' love. That prayer will be your anchor and your salvation."
Continue trying being virtuous if not, "sailing on the high seas can lead you to capsize and result in shipwreck."

DON'T WORRY.
DON'T BE ANXIOUS.
HUMBLY RECEIVE HIS
BODY AND BLOOD.

Compiled for Saint *Francis of Assisi*

LORD,

    make me an instrument of your peace:
    where there is hatred, let me sow love;
    where there is injury, pardon;
    where there is doubt, faith;
    where there is despair, hope;
    where there is darkness, light;
    where there is sadness, joy.

O divine Master, grant that I may not so much seek
to be consoled as to console,
to be understood as to understand,
to be loved as to love.

For it is in giving that we receive,
it is in pardoning that we are pardoned,
and it is in dying that we are born to eternal life.
Amen.

PEACE I leave with you, my peace I give to you, not as the world gives, do I give to you ... the peace which the world offers is a peace without tribulations ... peace without the cross is not the peace of Christ ... through many tribulations we must enter into the kingdom of God ... pray for "the grace of peace, so as not to lose that interior peace" ... "May the Lord help us to correctly understand this peace which he has given to us through the Holy Spirit".

Excerpts from Pope Francis' Daily Meditations:
"Tranquility" is not peace (16 May 2017)

LORD:

Give us the grace
to have interior peace.

Help us
to correctly understand
this peace
which was given to us
through the Holy Spirit.

AMEN.

Confer: Pope Francis' Daily Meditations - *"Tranquility" is not peace* (16 May 2017)

BE WITH
GOD'S PEACE
ALL WAYS
AND
ALWAYS!

P A X
et
BONUM

Saint (aka Padre Pio) Pius of Pietrelcina,
O.F.M. Cap. [Franciscan Capuchin]

PEACE
and
WELL-BEING.

Blessed Virgin Mary,
Mother of Prince of Peace,
QUEEN of PEACE,
pray for us.

Queen of Peace, stained glass; Monika Schappert

PEACE BE WITH YOU!

In the midst of the contradictions and perplexities we must confront each day, the din of so many words and opinions, there is the quiet voice of the Risen Lord who keeps saying to us:

"Peace be with you!

From the "Letter of His Holiness Pope Francis
to the Priests of the Diocese of Rome";
31 May 2020, the Solemnity of Pentecost.

**The voyage of life
has many storms.**

**Star of the Sea,
do not let us
be shipwrecked
in the tempest of war.***

**GO to
THE MERCY OCEAN
and find from it this:**

**EACE**

[* from the Act of Consecration of Russia and Ukraine to the
Immaculate Heart of Mary; Pope Francis, March 25, 2022]

FLEET ADMIRAL NIMITZ
and the
CHAPLAINS

"By his patient, sympathetic labors with the men, day in, day out, and through many a night, every chaplain I know contributed immeasurably to the moral courage of our fighting men. None of the effort appears in the statistics. Most of it was necessarily secret between pastor and his confidant. It is for that toil in the cause both of God and country that I honor the chaplain most."

Chester W. Nimitz, USN; May 1946

GO to
THE MERCY OCEAN ...

**for its marvelous depths
are beyond compare ...
for its everlasting Love ...**

~ ~~~~ ~~~~~~~~~ ~~~~~~ ~~~~~~~~~~~~~~~ ~~~~~~~~ ~~~

Confer: Psalm 107:23-32

SWIM in MERCY

SWIM
in
THE MERCY OCEAN

- even if not -

be immersed
through, and with, and in
trust to
DIVINE MERCY.

ACCLAIMS FOR *THE MERCY OCEAN*

"Fr. Salamoni's unique reflections on Faith and Life in a nautical context have always spoken to me and others who are involved in maritime work and the ministry to the People of the Sea. May this collection be an inspiration to all mariners, and all who live, recreate or work upon the vast waters." – **Doreen M Badeaux, Secretary General Apostleship of the Sea of the United States of America**

"I have served with Fr Salamoni for many years as a fellow Active Duty Navy Chaplain. I have been the beneficiary of his writings which were always joyful, thought provoking, and a delight to read. I heartily and happily give my endorsement to this latest collection. Enjoy!" – **Bishop Joseph L Coffey, Vicar for Veterans Affairs, Archdiocese for the Military Services, USA**

On the occasion of the 9/11 Boatlift 20th Anniversary Tribute: "Thank you Chaplain: We appreciate you thinking of us as we prepare to honor the heroes, victims and survivors. Your maritime-related prayers continue to uplift many of our members." – **Jessica LM Hitchen, Executive Director, New York Council Navy League**

"May *The Mercy Ocean* be a source of consolation for all who ponder on its gems of wisdom." — **Very Rev. Peter S. Kucer, MSA, STD; President-Rector of Holy Apostles College & Seminary.**

"To those who meditate, the Spirit's gift of Knowledge and Understanding is abundant, and the Heart of Jesus is open for us to see if we seek Him in such a path. Father Vincent's short work of collected meditations and memorable quotes from various sources is a simple and genuine fruit of his own labor of meditation. Enveloped in beautiful images, and even more beautiful thoughts, *The Mercy Ocean* is a piece meant to help those along their own path of meditation. Read slowly, read carefully, and read seeking the face of Jesus and the Immaculate Heart of Mary." — **Fra. Angelo, Knights of the Holy Eucharist**

"More than a sailor's retreat, Fr. Vincent Salamoni's *The Mercy Ocean* is a sailor's delight in the way it inspires the contemplative to cast out into the deep of God's mercy and grace." — **Dr. Sebastian Mahfood, OP, author of *The Narrative Spirituality of Dante's Divine Comedy: a hundred-day guided journal***

SUPPLEMENT
for
THE MERCY OCEAN

The QSR de TMO (unabridged) is not in *THE MERCY OCEAN,*
while it focused a concept into *THE MERCY OCEAN.*
It drifts, yet it ties in the same berth in *THE MERCY OCEAN.*

QSR de TMO

(unabridged)

[the title is explained]

What is the reason for the title QSR de TMO?

_____

QSR: The letters "QSR" represent the words:

Quiet, **S**ilence, and **R**est.
See the following pages.

_____

de: These letters recall the Saint Jane Frances de Chantal.
A quote of her is in following pages.

_____

TMO: The letters "TMO" are for a book's title:

The **M**ercy **O**cean.
The book's article SILENT HEART has QSR there.
And, the book's article SAINT DE CHANTAL and THE MERCY
OCEAN has an original paragraph below Saint Jane's quote.

_____

Try to be
QUIET.
Try
SILENCE
all inner noise,
and
REST
in God's Love.

Compiled from Pope Francis' Apostolic Journey to Mozambique.

**From a quote of
Saint Jane Frances de Chantal
and from
THE MERCY OCEAN.**

*"Sometimes put yourself very simply before God, certain of
his presence everywhere, and without any effort, whisper
very softly to His sacred heart whatever your own heart
prompts you to say."* - (Letters of Spiritual Direction)

———————

**Present in the Merciful Presence.
Present to the Sacred Heart
the encouragement was given.**

———————

Try to be
QUIET.
Present in the Merciful Presence.

Try
SILENCE
all inner noise,
Present to the Sacred Heart

and
REST
in God's Love.
the encouragement was given.

Compiled from Pope Francis' Apostolic Journey to Mozambique;
and from the section of Saint de Chantal in *The Mercy Ocean*.

PRESENT

PRESENCE

PRESENT*

* This page is an abridged compile of
Pope Francis' Apostolic Journey to Mozambique;
and from the section of
Saint de Chantal in the book *The Mercy Ocean*.

NEVER DIE!

**Old soldiers never die,
they simply fade away.
(from *Old Soldiers Never Die*)**

**Old sailor radarmen never die,
they fade away like a contact,
or pass their CPE.*
(from *Vincent A. Salamoni*)**

* (Closest Point of Approach)

"O Jesus,
the soul who plunges into
the shoreless ocean of Your Love,
draws with her
all the treasures she possesses."

**Story of a Soul
The Autobiography of
St. Thérèse of Lisieux; Chapter XI**

THE MERCY OCEAN

AMPLIFY

PRAYER
to the
HOLY SPIRIT

Come, Holy Spirit,
fill the hearts of your faithful
and enkindle in them the fire of your love.

[The stain glass is in St. Peter's Basilica, Vatican City, and the prayer is in the *Roman Missal*, Pentecost Sequence.]

THE "PROTO STAR"
for
THE MERCY OCEAN

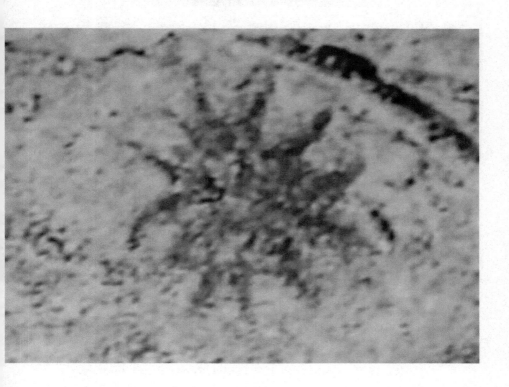

A detail from the oldest known picture of the Blessed Virgin Mary.

It is in the Catacomb of Priscilla, Rome, c. 3rd century.

The "star shall come out of Jacob" (Numbers 24:17).

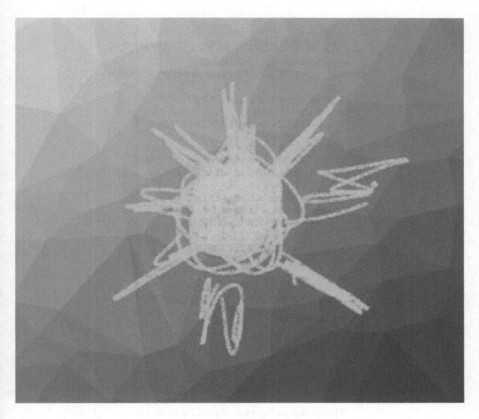

HEART
of
CHRIST'S MYSTICAL BODY
Commentary August 15-22, 2019

"(L)ook with mercy upon your people and especially upon the mystical body of your Church."

"Can anyone's heart remain closed and hardened after this?"

[From a dialogue On Divine Providence by Saint Catherine of Siena, virgin; (4, 13: ed. latina, Ingolstadii 1583, ff. 19v-20) / Liturgy of the Hours, 19 Sunday, Office of the Readings].

Of course, the first sentence refers of
Christ's Mystical Body.

Naturally, *the body includes the heart!*

HEART of CHRIST'S MYSTICAL BODY
Extraordinary Jubilee (2015/2016)
The concept was the first time to *emphasized* it!

If it was or never mentioned in the past,
in any event, now, it is a catalyst being:
UNITED in the LORD JESUS.

St. Catherine's other sentence wrote,
**"Can anyone's heart remain closed
and hardened after this?"**

**Can everyone's heart remain opened
and have a tender heart after
COMMUNICATE
YOUR
COMMENTARY?**

*   *   *   *   *   *

**THE HEART OF THE QUEEN,
WHO ASSUMED INTO HEAVEN,
PRAY FOR US.**

*   *   *   *   *   *

— —
Note:
St. Catherine's attributes include bearing a ship with the Papal coat of arms.

**This originally star was drawn from
Vincent A. Salamoni, Missionaries of the Holy Apostles (M.S.A.)
in the book
*The Mercy Ocean.***

**Furthermore, the star was in one of his article
*The lamp is the Lamb.***
**It illustrated in it as
the Star of Bethlehem / the Child's Star,
the Star of the Sea,
saints and yourself!**

(...) in which you shine like stars in the world.
(Philippians 2:15)

The lamp is the Lamb.

The Baptism of the Lord

This is a *catalyst*:

[The Epiphany of the Lord ∞ The Baptism of the Lord ∞ The Wedding of Cana]

Isaiah 42 _ a light for the nations.
Psalm 29 _ The Lord is over the waters /
the Lord is enthroned as king forever.
Acts of the Apostles 10 _ God shows no partiality / in every nation.
Luke 3 _ You are my beloved / with you I am well pleased.

The Magi guided from to star of the East.

**After the Nativity in Bethlehem,
their gifts were presented
to the Wedding of Cana!**

Time is a part of the creation.

Our journey have begun to eternity.

The history of these mysteries are partially unveiled here:

Epiphany:
(Morning Prayer, Canticle of Zechariah) **Today the Bridegroom claims his
bride, the Church, since Christ has washed her sins away in Jordan's
waters; the Magi hasten with their gifts to the royal wedding; and the
wedding guests rejoice, for Christ has changed water into wine, alleluia.**
(Evening Prayer II, Canticle of Mary) **Three mysteries mark this holy day:
today the star leads the Magi to the infant Christ; today water is changed
into wine for the wedding feast; today Christ wills to be baptized by John
in the river Jordan to bring us salvation.**
Saturday after Epiphany to the Baptism of the Lord:
(Divine Office, Second Reading) **(...) all these events at Cana are strange
and wonderful; to those who understand, they are also signs. For, if we look
closely, the very water tells us of our rebirth in baptism.**
2nd Sunday in Ordinary Time, John 2:1-11 [Cycle C]:
Jesus did this as the beginning of his signs at Cana in Galilee.

∞ 09 I 20

The MOTHER of GOD

is the source of all her titles.

**Words have limitations.
These "lifesaver" and "beacon"
are catalysts for devotion to her.**

The Magi from the East followed the Child's star.

**The Mother of God
has a title
STELLA MARIS | the STAR of the SEA.**

We follow her.

**In our lives,
we become overwhelm
in the waves of our lives.**

We look to her as a lifesaver for us.

**Our Mother is a beacon
beckons to:**

The lamp is the Lamb.

(Revelation 21:23)

Note:

The REASON for the IMMACULATE CONCEPTION
Mary's immaculate flesh knitted the blessed fruit of her womb!
(confer Psalm 139:13)

After the Nativity of the Lord,
the Magi's gifts were presented
to the Wedding of Cana!

Time is a measure.

In eternity there is no time.
With the Lord one day is like a thousand years,
and a thousand years are like one day.

The history of these mysteries are partially unveiled here:

The Star of Bethlehem and the Star of the Sea
are beacons that beckon to:
the lamp is the Lamb.

LAMB of GOD ... AGNUS DEI.

Thursday of the Third Week in Ordinary Week

This is a *catalyst*:

Gospel Acclamation Psalm 119:105
A lamp to my feet is your word,
a light to my path.

Mark 4:21-25
"Is a lamp brought in to be placed
under a bushel basket or under a bed,
and not to be placed on a lamp stand?
(...) nothing is secret except to come to light.

Communion Antiphon Cf. Psalm 34 (33):6
Look toward the Lord and be radiant;
let your faces not be abashed.
Or: John 8:12
I am the light of the world, says the Lord;
whoever follows me will not walk in darkness,
but will have the light of life.

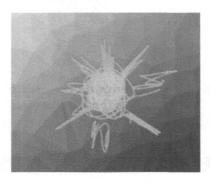

The lamp is the Lamb.

(Revelation 21:23)

LET US LOVE ONE ANOTHER.
Don't worry and don't be anxious.
Humbly receive Jesus' Body and Blood.
Lord, I am not worthy (...) and my soul shall be healed.

152

Follow and look for the
lamp is the Lamb,

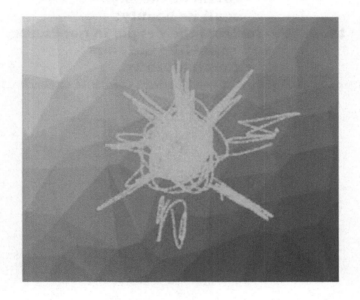

and be radiant;
so your faces
shall never be ashamed.

(Confer Revelation 21:23 and Psalm 34:5)

**Those who are learned will be as
radiant as the sky
in all its beauty;
those who instruct the people in goodness
will shine like the stars
for all eternity.**
(Common of Doctors of the Church; Canticle of Zechariah)

(...) in which you shine like stars in the world.
(Philippians 2:15)

TRUST GOD ... TRACK GOD

Plot both:

"In God We Trust ... All Others We Track."

"Track GOD."

The former trusts the Creator and mistrusts creatures.
The latter continues for the true course to the heavenly harbor.

Notes:
- The insignia is a rating badge; it symbolizes a radar scope.
- "Plot" with "track" - mark a route or position on a chart; a chart is a map for the use of navigators, to understand a movement.
- It would be as an example for discerning in the Mercy Ocean.
- The "former" is a popular expression; the "latter" is an original one.

SAINT AUGUSTINE and *THE MERCY OCEAN*

The great Doctor of the Church St. Augustine of Hippo spent over 30 years working on his treatise De Trinitate *[about the Holy Trinity], endeavoring to conceive an intelligible explanation for the mystery of the Trinity.*

The Vision of St. Augustine

St. Augustine was walking by the seashore one day contemplating the mystery of the Holy Trinity when he saw a little child running back and forth from the water to a spot on the seashore. The boy was using a shell to carry water from the large ocean and pour it into a small pit that he had made in the sand.

Augustine came up to him and asked him what he was doing.

"I'm going to pour the entire ocean into this hole," the boy replied.

"What?" said Augustine. "That is impossible, my dear child, the sea is so great and the shell and the hole are so little."

"That is true," the boy said. "It would be easier and quicker to draw all the water out of the sea and fit it into this hole than for you to fit the mystery of the Trinity and His Divinity into your little intellect; for the Mystery of the Trinity is greater and larger in comparison with your intelligence than is this vast ocean in comparison with this little hole."

And then the child vanished.

What does it mean?

Some say that St. Augustine had been talking with an angel sent by God to teach him a lesson on intellectual pride. Others say it was the Christ Child Himself who came to remind Augustine of the limits of human understanding in relation to the great mysteries of our Faith.

The Sea Shell
Because of this story,
the sea shell has become a symbol of St. Augustine and the study of theology.

The article above is based on the story in the "Golden Legend", written in A. D. 1275 by Jacobus de Voragine, Archbishop of Genoa via Our Lady of Mercy Lay Carmelite Community.

**Saint Augustine
contemplated the mystery of the Most Blessed Trinity.**

THE MERCY OCEAN

readers may pour that whole in another hole!*

* The hole is the One.

ART

and

THE MERCY OCEAN

Star of the Stormy Sea
by Mary Kloska

There are relationships,
with all the partakers in the

HEART
of
**CHRIST'S
MYSTICAL BODY.**

Here is an example, with only from a book's title:

**"A Heart Frozen in the Wilderness:
The Reflections of a Siberian Missionary".**

AGAIN:
**This is a catalyst
for YOU
to understand more
YOUR
part of the
HEART
of CHRIST'S MYSTICAL BODY!**

So here is the next page:

A Heart Frozen in the Wilderness:
The Reflections of a Siberian Missionary
by *Mary Kloska*

This writes about:
The Heart of a Child, the Russian Heart, Jesus' Patient Heart on the Cross, Our Lady's Immaculate Heart ...
It is a catalyst for YOUR part in the HEART of CHRIST'S MYSTICAL BODY. Others are being with or not with a heart frozen?
A "star of the stormy sea" in our lives, which is among frozen lakes, rivers, seas, even a merciless ocean, which was melting and warming from A HEART FROZEN.
YOU be shine like stars in the world (see Philippians 2:15)!

Our Lady, Star on the Sea
of Jesus' Mercy he is Our guiding Light and Life-raft to safety.
- by Mary Kloska; 2022

[Supplement]
The Canticle of the Creation
and
The Immaculate Conception and God's Plan*

PRIMACY of the UNIVERSE
Jesus is the culmination of the creation.
Jesus, is the King of the Universe.

The REASON

for the
IMMACULATE CONCEPTION
was because:

Mary's immaculate flesh knitted
the blessed fruit of her womb!

GOD'S PLAN
knitted me together in my mother's womb.
(confer Psalm 139:13)

The Blessed Virgin Mary
baby's Person
was
INCARNATED
from her
IMMACULATE FLESH.

The Second Person of the Most Holy Trinity
in the Incarnation Mystery
had perfect flesh.

*
"The Immaculate Conception and God's Plan" is an article from V. Salamoni, M.S.A.
Also, see an icon from Mary Kloska.

Our Lady,
Knitting as the Holy Spirit knits Jesus together
in Her womb because of Her Fiat.
- by Mary Kloska; 2022

"Saint Brendan and the Whale"
from a 15th-century manuscript.

OUR LADY of VICTORY

OUR LADY of the ROSARY

Those titles above are from the history of the Battle of Lepanto.
(1571)

Saint Pope Pius V
sent chaplains aboard the Christian ships.

This phrase became:
"Non virtus, non arma, non duces,
sed Mariae Rosarium victores nos fecit".

Neither valor, nor arms, nor leaders,
but the Rosary of Our Lady gave the victory.

30 April 2022
Saint Pius V, *optional memorial*
His papal coat of arms:

WALK ON THE SEA
CARRY YOUR CROSS
TAKE JESUS' YOKE

— — —

Y

C R O S S

W A L K

E

— — —

Jesus walking on the waters (cf. John 6:19).

In other scenes:

Jesus said, "If persons to become my followers, then deny and take your cross daily and follow me (cf. Luke 9:23).

"Come to me, all you that are weary and are carrying heavy burdens, and I will give you rest. Take my yoke upon/with you, and learn from me; for I am gentle and humble in heart, and you will find rest for your souls. For my yoke is easy, and my burden is light" (cf. Matthew 21:28-30).

Walk these paths
without footprints
through, with, in
THE MERCY OCEAN.

THE MERCY OCEAN
through, and with and in
The Lord of the Rings

This is with sprinkling grains of sea salt
(confer Matthew 5:13)
and a poetic license:

Neither seed cakes,
nor
hardtack
or even an anchovies pizza!

Take this:
the Bread of Angels,
all of you, and eat of it:

The lamp is the LAMB.
(Revelation 21:23)

25 III ∞

Anything to the contrary notwithstanding.

— — —

"Note" this song:

Mother Dear, O Pray for Me:
"I wander in a fragile bark,
O'er life's tempestuous sea (...) darkling waters flow (...)
Mother dear, remember me!"

— — —

(...) and the sea was no more.
(Revelation 21:1)

Blessed are the merciful,
for they will have mercy.
(Matthew 5:7)

Jesus, the King of the Universe is its Sea.
Confer Saint Padre Pio in the "Peace" section.

... Love continues.
(I Corinthians 13:13)

THE LOG

- 2015/2016 – Extraordinary Jubilee of Mercy – the articles start.
- 2020 – gathered in a collection with the title: THE MERCY OCEAN.
- August 15, 2021 – The Solemnity of the Assumption of the Blessed Virgin Mary; THE MERCY OCEAN was published.
- November 2021 – in the beginning of the month, there were pages added with these Saints: Peter, Vincent de Paul, Paul of the Cross, Boniface, John Bosco and Thérèse of Lisieux.
- November 2021 – after those additions, the page "Saint Vincent de Paul with Noah" was included.
- Nov. 13, 2021 – the phrase "In the one family of God has THE MERCY OCEAN ..." concluded the page "SAINT VINCENT de PAUL with NOAH". And another sentence was not in the book. In the event, it is in my heart and yours: THE MERCY OCEAN has a lifesaver for you!
- November 24, 2021 - the page concerning the anchor in Hebrew 6:19, included a quote from one of the Vietnamese Martyrs.
- Advent 2021 - the author draws the original "Stella" Maris | "Star" of the Sea. It is in the "STELLA MARIS ... *DEEP WATER*" section, in the Back Cover and here:

- Christmas Season 2021/2022 - the "STELLA MARIS ... *DEEP WATER*" section includes Saint Bonaventure, and the Blessed Virgin Mary is a lifesaver and beacon for our stormy seas. Also, Saint Thomas Becket presents.
- February 22, 2022, the Chair of Saint Peter, Apostle - the AMPLIFY includes the "PROTO" STAR for THE MERCY OCEAN, "The lamp is the Lamb" et cetera!

"After a dangerous voyage, at last I am in sight of the port I have been trying to get to for so long. I shall now be able to enjoy my God ... and I shall be freed from a heavy load which I just can't bear."
- Saint Louis of Anjou, on his deathbed

— — —

~~ ~~~~ ~~~~~~~~~~~~ ~~~~~~ ~~~~~~~~~~~~~~~~~ ~~~~~~~~~ ~~~

Vincent A. Salamoni
><> ><> ><> ><> ><> ><> ><> ><> ><> ><> ><> ><>

The articles start in 2015/2016 at the Extraordinary Jubilee of Mercy.
Dedicated:
Our Lady, Star of the Sea
Last Thursday of September 2022

Made in the USA
Columbia, SC
14 October 2022

69488059R00095